CONCEALED CARRY REVOLUTION

Expanding the Right to Bear Arms in America

DAVID YAMANE

ISBN 978-1-9701-0937-5

Published March 2021
Berkeley, CA

A N E W P R E S S

TABLE OF CONTENTS

PREFACE

Despite the profound significance of the issue, no comprehensive but concise history of concealed carry laws in the United States yet exists. *Concealed Carry Revolution* seeks to fill this gap. This small book was originally written as a chapter in the larger book on Gun Culture 2.0 on which I continue to work. As the chapter grew longer and the focus of that work shifted, I found myself with a great deal of material which had no obvious outlet. The idea of self-publishing came to me as I saw others being able to quickly get their ideas into the public square in a more composed and coherent manner than a blog. Among my fellow scholars, self-publishing is undoubtedly looked down upon, but it seems to me like the perfect vehicle for a work such as this.

To satisfy the interests of experts, but maintain readability for interested others, I have put as much documentation and nuance as possible in the end notes. The source of quotes and observations in the text that are not documented in the notes are from interviews and fieldwork (in person and mediated) that I have conducted as part of my ongoing research on American gun culture. For those interested in learning more about the broader project, please visit either of my blogs: gunculture2point0.com or guncurious.com. Some of my peer-reviewed scholarly publications on the topic are listed in note 7.

My intellectual debts are too numerous to list here, but are reflected in part in the end notes and individuals I quote in the text. I am grateful for editorial input provided by Kelly Sunshine and production assistance by 2Nimble. I could not have done this work without financial support from a Reynolds Research Leave and a grant from the Social, Behavioral, and Economic Sciences Research Fund at Wake Forest University. More recently, various individuals have supported this work by making small donations through my "Buy Me a Coffee" page (https://www.buymeacoffee.com/gunculture2pt0). Those who sign up as monthly or annual members are receiving a free copy of this book as a "Thank You!" gift.

Introduction

TOMBSTONE AND DODGE CITY, THEN AND NOW

"There is no one here but carries arms under his clothes."

— Montgomery, Alabama lawyer
to Alexis de Tocqueville in 1832

It is far easier for a private citizen to carry a concealed firearm in Dodge City, Kansas or Tombstone, Arizona today than it was in the 19th century. Contrary to popular perceptions cultivated by television programs like *Gunsmoke* and movies like *Gunfight at the O.K. Corral*, these legendary towns on the American frontier had strict regulations on the bearing of arms.

Two days after the Kansas legislature authorized the organization of Ford County in 1874, "the county commissioners passed their first measure aimed at the suppression of violence at the county seat with a resolution 'that any person found carrying concealed weapons in the city of Dodge or violating the laws of the State shall be dealt with according to law.'" An 1876 city ordinance further clarified that "any person who shall in the City of Dodge City, *carry concealed*, or *otherwise*, about his or her person, any *pistol, bowie knife, sling shot*, or other *dangerous* or *deadly weapon*, except United States Civil Officers, State, County, Township or City officers shall be fined . . . *Seventy-Five* Dollars." The essence of these laws is captured in a famous 1879 photograph of a sign on Front Street in Dodge City that suggests visitors "TRY Prickly Ash BITTERS," and above that declares, "The Carrying of Fire Arms STRICTLY PROHIBITED."[1]

Not long after the Dodge City photograph was taken, the Tombstone, Arizona city council passed a law banning the carrying of deadly weapons. Ordinance No.9, "To Provide against Carrying of

Deadly Weapons" became effective in April 1881.
It read:

> Section 1. It is hereby declared unlawful to carry
> in the hand or upon the person or otherwise any
> deadly weapon within the limits of said city of
> Tombstone, without first obtaining a permit in
> writing.
>
> Section 2: This prohibition does not extend to
> persons immediately leaving or entering the city,
> who, with good faith, and within reasonable time
> are proceeding to deposit, or take from the place of
> deposit such deadly weapon.
>
> Section 3: All fire-arms of every description, and
> bowie knives and dirks, are included within the
> prohibition of this ordinance.

Whether one believes the ordinance was passed in the
interest of public safety or because of a feud between
town Marshal Virgil Earp with his clan and the McLaury
and Clanton brothers, it is clear that the ordinance
precipitated the famous October 1881 shootout at the
OK Corral. When Virgil and Morgan Earp arrested Ike
Clanton, it was for violating Tombstone's Ordinance
No. 9 – the "Earp Ordinance," as it came to be known.[2]

In the O.K. Corral theme park area of Tombstone, Arizona re-enactors relive the "Town Too Tough To Die" days of the 1880s, when western gunfighters such as Wyatt Earp and John Henry "Doc" Holliday swaggered along the streets of town

Credit: Library of Congress, Prints & Photographs Division, photograph by Carol M. Highsmith (2018663346)

The ability to carry guns lawfully in public in the 21st century could not be more different from the situation in the 19th century. Arizona's 1912 State Constitution included Art. II, § 26: "The right of the individual citizen to bear arms in defense of himself or the State shall not be impaired, but nothing in this section shall be construed as authorizing individuals or corporations to organize, maintain, or employ an armed body of men." This was widely interpreted to allow open carry of firearms by anyone who could legally possess one, although the "Earp Ordinance" remained not only on the books in Tombstone, but was also enforced into the 1990s when it was finally challenged in court. In

1994, Arizona adopted a concealed carry system that maintained anyone in the state who meets the statutory requirements shall be issued a permit. According to the state Department of Public Safety, over 378,000 permits were active in fall 2020, representing 5.2 percent of the state population. Beginning in 2010, Arizona became the third state to allow residents to carry concealed weapons without a permit (following Vermont, which has never required any permit, and Alaska, whose law took effect in 2003). Called "Constitutional Carry" or "Freedom to Carry" by its proponents, this permitless carry system allows anyone who can legally own a firearm also to carry it concealed in public, including in most parts of Tombstone.[3]

Kansas was slower to liberalize its gun carry laws than Arizona but followed a similar pattern. In 2006, the legislature adopted the Kansas Personal and Family Protection Act, which established shall issue concealed carry in the state. The law held that individuals without disqualifying conditions, such as an adjudicated mental defect or conviction of a misdemeanor crime of domestic violence, will receive their license to carry within 90 days from when they complete an 8-hour weapons safety and training course from a state-certified instructor, submit their applications (including a photograph and fingerprinting) to the sheriff in their county of residence, and pay their fees to the county sheriff ($32.50) and Kansas Attorney General ($100).

From 2007 through 2014, Kansas issued over 94,000 permits. This included 694 in Ford County, about 2 percent of the population of the still sparsely populated home to Dodge City. In April of 2015, Kansas joined Vermont, Alaska, Arizona, Wyoming, and Arkansas in allowing residents who are not otherwise excluded under federal or state law to carry concealed handguns in most public places without a permit.[4]

The difference between Dodge City and Tombstone in the 1880s and those cities in the 2010s is enlightening in several ways. First, restrictions on carrying firearms in the 19th century were widespread, even in places we associate with a strong gun culture. *Especially* in those places, in fact. As Constitutional law professor Adam Winkler concludes in his book, *Gunfight: The Battle over the Right to Bear Arms in America*, "The Shootout at the O.K. Corral . . . is not only a story about America's gun culture. It is a tale about America's gun *control* culture."[5] Significant restrictions on carrying concealed weapons beginning in the American South in the early 1800s spread throughout the country and remained in place well into the 20th century.

Second, perhaps as surprising to many as the restrictiveness of gun laws in the Wild West is the fact that the federal government in the United States passed no laws concerning firearms for nearly 150 years, from the nation's inception to the 1934 National Firearms

Act. The most interesting and important developments in terms of gun laws have always taken place at the state level.[6]

Third, since the late 1970s, a movement for concealed carry rights, combined with favorable court rulings, has dramatically reversed the historic pattern of restriction on gun carrying beginning in the early 1800s. Permitless carry is the frontier of these laws, but liberal laws permitting concealed carry are now firmly entrenched in a majority of states. Of course, with these state laws, the devil is in the details, as we will see. Local differences notwithstanding, the recent history of the United States has seen an unprecedented liberalization of gun laws leading to a dramatic expansion in the right to bear arms. These developments reflect and facilitate what I call, following Michael Bane, Gun Culture 2.0.[7]

One

THE RESTRICTED ERA OF GUN CARRY

The governments of Dodge City and Tombstone did not invent restrictions on the right to keep and bear arms. From the very origin of this Anglo-American right, there were limitations. William Blackstone's famous "Commentaries on the Laws of England" identified "having and using arms for self-preservation and defense" as the fifth auxiliary right of British subjects (auxiliary to natural rights of personal security, personal liberty, and private property). Yet the English

Bill of Rights of 1689 both codified and proscribed that right: "That the subjects which are Protestants may have arms for their defence suitable to their conditions and as allowed by law." The right in the first place extended only to property-owning, male Protestants.

The same was true in the British Colonies. The Massachusetts Bay Colony barred some 100 colonists from owning guns in 1637 because, as followers of religious nonconformists Anne Hutchinson and John Wheelwright, they were thought to be heretics. Other categories of individuals banned from exercising gun rights in Colonial America were non-property-owning whites, indentured servants, and both free negroes and slaves.[8] Along with ownership, the use of guns was also limited, as in a 1713 law prohibiting firing a gun in the mainland part of Boston. These restrictions notwithstanding, the affirmation of the right to keep and bear arms in the Second Amendment to the United States Constitution both reflected and supported the widespread ownership of guns.

As Clayton Cramer argued in response to the subsequently disgraced historian Michael Bellesiles, "Gun ownership appears to have been the norm for freemen, and not terribly unusual for free women and at least male children, through the Colonial, Revolutionary, and early Republic periods." Guns played a fundamental role "for the collective military purposes of each colony; for the defense of individual families and isolated settlements; as symbols of being a citizens with the duty to defend the society; and more than occasionally, to demonstrate that nothing has changed in the human condition since Cain slew Abel." With ownership came abuse, not just of guns but also of other weapons. In 1832, a lawyer in Montgomery, Alabama told the famous French observer of American society Alexis de Tocqueville, "There is no one here but carries arms under his clothes. At the slightest quarrel, knife or pistol comes to hand. These things happen continually; it is a semi-barbarous state of society." When Alabama finally banned the carrying of concealed weapons in 1839, it was not a pioneer but the eighth state to do so.[9]

A quarter-century earlier, in 1813, the Commonwealth of Kentucky passed the nation's first law prohibiting the carrying of concealed weapons. The General Assembly of the Commonwealth determined:

> That any person in this commonwealth, who shall hereafter wear a pocket pistol, dirk, large knife, or sword in a cane, concealed as a weapon, unless when travelling on a journey, shall be fined in any sum, not less than one hundred dollars; . . . One half of such fine shall be to the use of the informer, and the other to the use of the commonwealth.

However, nine years later, a resident of the Commonwealth challenged the law in court and succeeded. In 1822, the Kentucky Supreme Court ruled the concealed weapons ban violated the state's 1792 Constitution: "That the rights of the citizens to bear arms in defense of themselves and the State shall not be questioned." Consequently, Kentucky's Constitutional Convention in 1849 amended the state's original constitutional language to add the clause: "but the General Assembly may pass laws to prevent persons from carrying concealed arms." This allowed the state to ban the carrying of concealed weapons. Kentucky's ban remained in place for nearly 150 years, until 1996, when the state legislature passed a shall issue concealed carry law.[10]

In the time between Kentucky's original 1813 ban and Alabama's in 1839, six other states passed concealed weapon bans: Louisiana (1813), Indiana (1820), Georgia (1837), Arkansas (1837-38), Tennessee (1838), and Virginia (1838). Most observers of the contemporary United States see the South as being the heart of American gun culture. At first glance, therefore, it would seem odd that seven of the first eight states to restrict concealed carry were southern. In his unique history, *Concealed Weapon Laws of the Early Republic*, Clayton Cramer reviews and dismisses a number of explanations for the rise of these laws, including slavery, higher average climatic temperatures, and urbanization. He concludes that the main impetus to limit the right to carry concealed weapons was the harmful effects of the backcountry culture of violence found especially in the southern United States.[11]

THE DUEL.

Woodcut of "The Duel" (1834) showing Andrew Jackson killing Charles Dickenson
Credit: Library of Congress, Prints & Photographs Division, Illustration in: Major Jack Downing's Life of Andrew Jackson (2005683543)

In this culture, people were expected to resort to personal violence to resolve minor disputes, and especially insults to their honor. In some cases, efforts to suppress dueling as a means of resolving personal disputes had an unintended consequence of promoting more spontaneous interpersonal violence, which the concealed weapon laws were then designed to counteract. According to Kentucky historian Robert Ireland,

When the duel was legal, men did not need to arm themselves because they knew that the formal mechanisms of the duel were available to resolve affairs of honor. Thus, sudden quarrels seldom produced immediate bloodshed because so few men habitually armed themselves. With the outlawing of the duel, cowards began to wear concealed arms since they no longer had to worry about social ostracism if they used their concealed weapons to surprise and unfairly take advantage of their adversaries. Courageous gentleman followed suit to protect themselves from cowardly assassination.

It is worth noting that the practice of openly carrying weapons was considered acceptable and even honorable. The problem was concealment. In 1850, the Louisiana Supreme Court reasoned:

> This law became absolutely necessary to counteract a vicious state of society, growing out of the habit of carrying concealed weapons, and to prevent bloodshed and assassinations committed upon unsuspecting persons. It interfered with no man's right to carry arms (to use its words) 'in full open view,' which places men upon an equality. This is the right guaranteed by the Constitution of the United States, and which is calculated to incite men to a manly and noble defense of themselves,

if necessary, and of their country, without any tendency to secret advantages and unmanly assassinations.

The Court's reasoning for upholding the statute making concealed carry a misdemeanor in Louisiana expressed a widely held sentiment.[12]

Of course, then as now, legally prohibiting a behavior and eliminating that behavior from society are far from equivalent. Reflecting on his time as a police officer in Tennessee in the 1970s, gun trainer Tom Givens says it was so common for people to carry guns in their cars that when he pulled someone over he did not ask, "Do you have a gun in your car?" He asked, "Where is the gun in your car?" The existence of laws against some behavior is not the same as people following or officials enforcing those laws. This is especially true when there is a strong motivation to engage in the prohibited behavior (recall "Prohibition" in the United States). So, if the late 19th century was part of the restricted era, it was also, in the words of historians Lee Kennett and Jules LaVerne Anderson, "a gun-toting era."[13]

Kennett and Anderson's book, *The Gun in America: The Origins of a National Dilemma*, explains gun carrying both in terms of exigency and the normal course of daily life in the city. Urban areas grew dramatically in size over the course of the 19th century, but "everyday law enforcement did not keep pace." As a result, "the inhabitant felt an increased need to fend for himself in this regard. The sense of personal insecurities in the face of crime probably did more to foster the trend toward personal armament than anything else, with sporadic outbreaks of mass violence accelerating the process from time to time." To take but one example that is reminiscent of the events of 2020, in 1877 the *Chicago Tribune* reported that during that year's riots in the city, "every man who could beg, buy, or borrow a revolver carried it," with total disregard to the local ordinance against concealed weapons. Kennett and Anderson also report the results of a *New York Tribune* survey in 1903 that indicated "quite clearly that honest citizens often went armed. Those who traveled at night or with sums of money felt much safer with revolvers in their pockets. ... Most felt they needed them for self-defense, holding that the public guardians of the peace could not always be relied upon to protect life and property." As with today, when seconds counted, police were just minutes away.[14]

The reality of gun-toting notwithstanding, after a hiatus for the Civil War, laws banning concealed weapons spread to the rest of the South as part of Reconstruction. From Southern states, they radiated outward to the rest of the country.

Two

Discretionary, May Issue Carry Permitting Systems

New York State's 1866 concealed weapons law forbade the carrying of a diverse range of weapons, including "sling shot, billy, sand-club or metal knuckles and any dirk or dagger, or sword cane or air gun." Significantly, pistols were not on the list. In the following decade, the New York City Board of Alderman failed to approve a concealed carry permitting system for handguns "on the grounds that only respectable citizens would be affected." Prior to the 20ᵗʰ century, carrying concealed firearms was not a major social or political issue in New York.[15]

As historians Lee Kennett and James LaVerne Anderson observe, "Until the end of the century, the press tended to treat pistol-carrying in a quasi-humorous fashion, as though it were more a whimsy than a serious menace." They recount such an essay published in the *New York Tribune* in 1892 on "that pleasing American custom of carrying deadly weapons" practiced by "a very fair percentage" of New Yorkers:

> "Let a mad dog, for instance, take a turn around Times Square, and the spectator is astonished to see the number of men who will produce firearms from some of that multitude of pockets with which man, as constructed by the tailor, is endowed." Of one hundred men who fired at the dog, the *Tribune* continued, ninety-nine would miss, and one in ten would put a bullet through a bystander's leg, for "the average New Yorker who carries a pistol cannot hit anything with it."

Concern over guns in general, including "the general promiscuous toting of guns," increased dramatically in the 20ᵗʰ century.[16]

Recognizing the need to allow certain people to carry concealed weapons, states with carry bans developed laws that allowed sheriffs, police chiefs, or judges to issue concealed carry permits. A highly influential model for the restriction of concealed carry in the Northern states in the early 20th century was New York's 1911 Sullivan Act. Promoted by Timothy D. "Big Tim" Sullivan in the wake of an ongoing crime wave and the attempted assassination of New York City Mayor William Gaynor in 1910, the Act required a government issued license in order to possess and carry a pistol. To receive a license, the applicant needed to show evidence of "good moral character" and "proper cause." These highly (and intentionally) subjective criteria allowed a great deal of discretion in who authorities would permit to carry legally.[17]

The fact that measures like the Sullivan Act were being passed at the state level is significant, since the level of professionalization of state legislatures has not always been high. Indeed, one observer wrote in 1889, "it need scarcely be said that the State legislatures are not high-toned bodies."[18] Efforts to professionalize state legislatures included a movement toward the standardization of state laws in general. Consequently, in the 1920s and 30s a number of states adopted gun restrictions based on a model law called the "Uniform Act to Regulate the Sale and Possession of Firearms."

Politician Timothy ("Big Tim") Sullivan (right) with his half-brother Larry Mulligan returning to New York on the Imperator from a trip to England in 1913.

Credit: Library of Congress, Prints & Photographs Division, George Grantham Bain Collection (LC-B2- 2768-7)

The National Conference of Commissioners on Uniform State Laws created the Uniform Firearms Act based on a draft produced by the United States Revolver Association (USRA). The USRA saw its law as a way of preempting the passage of more severe gun control laws modeled on New York's Sullivan Law. It accepted the prohibition on carrying concealed pistols without a license in order to avoid the more severe requirement of needing a permit merely to own a gun. Among the states adopting versions of the Uniform Firearms Act were California, North Dakota, New Hampshire, Michigan, Connecticut, New Jersey, Rhode Island, Massachusetts,

Hawaii, and Oregon. These gun control measures were supported by "traditional gun culture" – hunters, target shooters, and other sporting firearms owners – and their voluntary associations, including the National Rifle Association. According to Brian Anse Patrick's history of the concealed carry movement, "Traditional gun culture... saw no problem whatsoever with outlawing general concealed carry ... As long as the interests of target shooters, sportsmen, and 'reputable' members of the public who wanted firearms for home or self-defense were preserved, all was good."[19]

In effect, where government authorities allowed concealed carry at all, it was under a discretionary system. Today we call these types of laws "may issue," meaning the permitting authority is not required to grant a permit but *may* do so at its discretion.[20] May issue laws continue to exist today in nine states: California, Connecticut,[21] Delaware, Hawaii, Maryland, Massachusetts, New Jersey, New York, Rhode Island.

How much discretion authorities in these states exercise varies, but low permitting rates in may issue states today suggest they frequently exercise this discretion to deny permits to carry. Nationwide, 7.6 percent of the total adult population has a concealed carry permit. Not including California and New York, 9.2 percent of American adults has a permit. In the nine may issue states, permitting rates range from a low of 0.00 percent in Hawaii to a high of 9.57 percent in Connecticut. The average permitting rate of 2.30 percent in these may issue states is less than one-third of the national rate.[22]

The twin towers of discretion in may issue permitting systems have always been the requirements that applicants be of "good moral character" and that they show "good cause" for needing to carry a gun. California's current statutory language provides an excellent example of this discretionary system (emphasis added):

California Penal Code Section 26150. (a) When a person applies for a license to carry a pistol, revolver, or other firearm capable of being concealed upon the person, the sheriff of a county *may issue* a license to that person upon proof of all of the following:

(1) The applicant is of *good moral character*.

(2) *Good cause* exists for issuance of the license.

(3) The applicant is a resident of the county or a city within the county, or the applicant's principal place of employment or business is in the county or a city within the county and the applicant spends a substantial period of time in that place of employment or business.

(4) The applicant has completed a course of training as described in Section 26165.

As one might expect, "good" moral character and "good" cause are highly subjective. "Good character" has often been a euphemism for being a celebrity, rich, politically connected, or all of the above. To wit: The list of individuals who have received gun permits in New York City under the still-in-effect Sullivan Law reads like an episode of *Lifestyles of the Rich and Famous*: Eleanor Roosevelt, Nelson Rockefeller, Arthur Ochs Sulzberger (publisher of the *New York Times*), Leland DuPont, Sammy Davis Jr., Robert Goulet, Bill Cosby, and Joan Rivers, among others. Cruising past flyover country to the left coast we find the Office of the Sheriff of Santa Clara County currently being investigated for what *The Mercury News* calls "a well-oiled patronage system with Santa Clara County concealed-gun permits." The article claims it was an "open secret . . . that political supporters of [Sheriff Laurie] Smith received special treatment from her agency," notably in the issuance of carry permits.[23]

In terms of ferreting out the good people who actually need to carry guns, Delaware's current process has some unique elements. First, an applicant needs to file with the issuing authority "a certificate of 5 respectable citizens of the county in which the applicant resides at the time of filing the application." Each of the five certificates from these "respectable citizens" – character references, in effect – must "clearly state that the applicant is a person of full age, sobriety and good moral character, that the applicant bears a good reputation for peace and good order in the community in which the applicant resides, and that the carrying of a concealed deadly weapon by the applicant is necessary for the protection of the applicant or the applicant's property, or both." In addition, the Superior Court of Delaware (which is responsible for issuing permits) includes the following in its instructions for an initial permit:

> Arrange With a Newspaper of General Circulation in Your County (Newspaper selection must have a circulation of at least 35 percent of the population in your zip code.)
>
> - Have your application published once, at least (10) business days before the filing of your application.
>
> - Obtain an affidavit from the newspaper company stating that this requirement has been met.
>
> - Attach the newspaper company's affidavit to your application.
>
> - Be sure to use your whole name – no initials – and your home address.

Presumably this is to allow fellow citizens to object to a person's application for a permit, but it is also clearly a general disincentive to apply. Not surprisingly, given these requirements, only 21,315 of Delaware's residents (2.77%) have permits to carry concealed weapons in the state.[24]

In some cases, no cause is good enough for an ordinary citizen to obtain a license. In the early 1980s, well-known Denver talk-show host Alan Berg applied for a carry permit from Denver Police Chief Ari Zavaras because of death threats he received from white supremacists due to his outspoken liberal views. Zavaras had issued very few permits, only to those who his office had determined had "true and compelling need." But what constituted true and compelling need? According to Zavaras's deputy in charge of permitting, "Just because you fear for your life is not a compelling reason to have a permit." Thus, Zavaras denied Berg a concealed carry permit. Members of the white nationalist organization, The Order, subsequently shot Berg dead in his driveway.[25]

The San Francisco Sheriff's Department also administers a "no cause is good cause" system. Although the department accepts applications for carry permits, in 2013 the Senior Deputy Sheriff responsible for concealed carry permits told me, "The Sheriff has not issued one in the two years I have been doing this job."

The fact that the Sheriff even has a process for accepting applications is only due to legal pressure brought to bear on the previous sheriff, Michael Hennessey, by the Calguns Foundation, a non-profit that advocates for gun rights in the state. James Harrigan, legal counsel to the Sheriff of San Francisco, acknowledged that a written policy for San Francisco "does not exist since they are never issued." Harrigan further explained, "Sheriff Hennessey has not, in twenty-two years as the elected Sheriff of San Francisco, issued a permit to any applicant to carry a concealed weapon. His position is fairly well known."[26] This level of discretion is perfectly legal under California's may issue concealed carry statute. As practiced in San Francisco, it is effectively an outright ban.[27]

On the other hand, some issuing authorities in California interpret "good cause" very liberally, such that anyone who wants to carry a concealed weapon for personal protection can get a permit. These jurisdictions, especially in the less populated areas of northern and central California, are *de facto* shall issue. An example is the Tehama County Sheriff's Office, which declares on its web page, "Sheriff-Coroner Dave Hencratt supports the right of law-abiding citizens to keep and bear arms. In this regard, all qualified residents of Tehama County are eligible to apply for a permit to carry concealed weapons." Shasta County, in far northern California like Tehama, is another example. At the end of 2014, there were 5,906 active civilian permits issued by the county sheriff, one for every 30 adult residents, the highest county rate in the state.[28]

Other California counties are more conservative, requiring applicants to meet a higher standard of good cause, called "heightened" good cause by some gun rights advocates. The modifier "heightened" appears nowhere in the law, but these county sheriffs look for some cause beyond simple personal protection, such as having been a victim of a crime, having a demonstrable credible threat of violence against you, carrying large amounts of money or valuables for work, or working late hours in a high crime rate area. San Mateo County (in the San Francisco Bay Area) is an example, with just 182 active permits issued by the sheriff through the end of 2014, one for every 3,700 or so adult residents of the county. In addition to San Francisco and San Mateo Counties, most of the counties in the San Francisco Bay Area, and counties to the south such as Los Angeles and Orange are very close to *de facto* no issue. Getting a permit is the exception rather than the rule. These are the most populous areas of the state, geographically arrayed along the coast from wine country to the border of Mexico.[29]

The may issue as *de facto* no issue practice along the blue coast of California is a legacy of the practice of restricting concealed carry begun in the early 1800s in the Bluegrass State of Kentucky. As Brian Anse Patrick observes, this process was largely completed by the 1930s: "legal concealed gun carrying in most American states had become a privilege of the few." Outright bans or strict discretionary systems were the status quo for concealed carry in most of the United States until the 1980s. This restricted era of gun carry, supported by traditional gun culture and upheld in court, continued until a new gun culture was energized beginning in the 1970s and gave rise to a new, more liberal era of gun carry.[30]

Three

THE RISE OF SHALL ISSUE CONCEALED CARRY

As a middle ground between complete bans and no restrictions on carrying, may issue laws in practice have tilted more toward bans. An alternative permitting system that leans more toward no restrictions is "shall issue" concealed carry. Although these permits still come with a number of strings attached, the issuing authority has little to no discretion in determining who is eligible to receive them. Any person who meets the statutory requirements *shall* be issued a permit. Prior to Florida's passage of shall issue concealed carry in the mid-1980s, only a few states made it relatively easy for an ordinary citizen to carry a concealed weapon legally.

Tumbler with parody of Starbucks logo, "I Love Guns & Coffee"
Credit: Photo courtesy of Tracy Thronburg Becker

Having adopted the gun-controlling Uniform Pistol and Revolver Act in 1935, Washington became the first state to reverse course when in 1961 it "required that if the applicant for a concealed weapon permit was allowed to possess a handgun under Washington law, the permit had to be issued."[31] For those who equate the State of Washington with the City of Seattle – the latter with its current reputation for Starbucks-drinking, REI-wearing, Microsoft-rich liberals – this would seem an unlikely location for the nation's first shall issue permitting system. However, the area's transformation into the "San Francisco of the Northwest" is actually fairly recent. Even today, one need not go far outside of Seattle proper to find a robust gun culture. Then, as now, much of the state was very rural, with strong hunting traditions and not a little strain of libertarianism.

Washington's early shall issue law also occasioned the first empirical study of concealed weapon permits. In "Law-Abiding One-Man Armies," sociologist Lawrence Northwood, social worker Richard Westgard, and civil engineer Charles Barb, Jr. examined why individuals applied for concealed weapon permits in Seattle in 1972. The authors estimated that 2.4 percent of Seattle's adult population of 363,000 at the time was law-abiding one-man armies. During the study period, from February through August 1972, the Seattle Police Department received 2,400 permit applications. Of those applicants, 90 percent were male, with a median age in the mid-40s for both men and women. Interestingly, in terms of racial self-identification, 79 percent of applicants said white, 16 percent black, and 5 percent other. As black residents made up only

7 percent of Seattle's population, they were over-represented among applicants for concealed weapon permits. This was due in part to the geographic concentration of gun permit applicants in three neighborhoods in which black residents were over-represented, and in part to the higher levels of victimization and anticipated victimization reported by black applicants. Liberalizing concealed carry laws in Washington allowed more racial minorities – and women, and especially minority women – in Seattle to take steps they felt necessary to protect themselves against actual and perceived threats.[32]

Washington's change did not spark any broader movement for liberalization of concealed carry laws in other states. It was not until 1980, almost two decades later, that Indiana became the next state to go shall issue (see Table 1).[33] By this time, major changes were taking place in the gun culture and the concealed carry movement was gaining strength.

The movement for and passage of the 1968 Gun Control Act, the first major federal firearms legislation since the Federal Firearms Act of 1938, politically activated the modern gun rights cause. The famous "Revolt at Cincinnati" embodied and furthered this political activism. At the National Rifle Association's 1977 annual meeting in Cincinnati, activists wrestled control of the organization from the old guard and directed it toward a more hardline stance regarding the right of all individual citizens to keep and bear arms. This, in conjunction with a dramatic rise in crime beginning in the 1960s, furthered the movement away from hunting and traditional target shooting as the core of American gun culture (Gun Culture 1.0), toward a gun culture centered on self-defense (Gun Culture 2.0). This created considerable momentum for passage of shall issue concealed carry laws at the state level in the 1980s.[34]

Following Indiana in 1980 were Maine, North Dakota, and South Dakota, all of which adopted shall issue concealed carry permitting systems in 1985. But the epicenter of the quake that would radiate across the country was Florida. The passage of Florida's shall issue law was the culmination of years of effort led by Marion Hammer, a lobbyist for the United Sportsmen of Florida. (Hammer also served as the first female president of the National Rifle Association from 1995 to 1998.) The Florida legislature first passed a shall issue concealed carry law in 1985, but it was vetoed by Democratic Governor Bob Graham. So it was not until 1987 that Republican Governor Bob Martinez signed shall issue concealed carry into law.

Table 1. State Adoption of Shall Issue Concealed Carry Laws

Year	States
1961	State of Washington
1980	Indiana
1985	Maine, North Dakota, South Dakota
1986	Utah
1987	Florida
1988	Pennsylvania
1989	Oregon, West Virginia, Georgia[35]
1990	Idaho
1991	Louisiana, Mississippi, Montana
1994	Alaska, Arizona, New Hampshire,[36] Tennessee, Wyoming
1995	Arkansas, Nevada, North Carolina, Oklahoma, Texas, Virginia
1996	Kentucky, South Carolina
2001	Michigan, New Mexico
2003	Colorado, Minnesota, Missouri
2004	Ohio
2006	Kansas, Nebraska
2010	Iowa
2011	Wisconsin
2013	Alabama, Illinois

Note: Dates in this table are from my own research and Trent Steidley, "Sharing the Monopoly on Violence? Shall-Issue Concealed Handgun License Laws and Responsibilization," *Sociological Perspectives* (2019), Table 1.

Although Florida did not create shall issue concealed carry, it did open the floodgates for a massive expansion in the number of states with liberalized concealed carry laws. Four other states passed shall issue laws in the three years following Florida: Pennsylvania in 1988, Oregon and West Virginia in 1989, and Idaho in 1990. Including Vermont, by 1990 a baker's dozen states had laws favoring the right-to-carry concealed weapons by ordinary citizens.[37] By the turn of the 21st century, more than half of the 50 states had liberalized their concealed weapon laws, and from 2001 to 2013, an additional 12 states followed suit.[38]

Just over 100 years after New York passed the influential may issue Sullivan Law, 40 out of 50 states had adopted liberalized concealed carry laws under which officials could not deny a permit to a citizen as long as that citizen met certain basic requirements. The movement for shall issue concealed carry has resulted in nearly 20 million citizens being permitted to bear arms concealed in public (and countless others being allowed to do so in permitless carry states).[39] But within this overall trend toward liberalization, substantial diversity exists among the shall issue states. All shall issue laws are not created equal.

Four

THE SHALL ISSUE DEVIL IS IN THE DETAILS

The broad principal that any citizen who meets the established criteria *shall* be issued a concealed weapon permit is a significant departure from the restricted era of carry that characterized American history from the mid-1800s to the 1980s. But for proponents of the Second Amendment right to keep and bear arms, the distinction between "rights" and "permits" is important. In the case of *rights*, the citizen possesses something upon which the government cannot infringe. In the case of *permits*, the government grants permission to a citizen to do something, and specifies the how, when, and where the citizen can do it. Consequently, even in the 40 more liberal concealed carry states, the process of receiving a permit and the conditions under which permit holders can carry vary greatly. Most concealed weapons permits come with many restrictions. As is often the case, the devil is in details.

Consider Illinois's permitting system, for example. When the U.S. Seventh Circuit Court of Appeals overturned the state's ban on public carrying of firearms in December 2012, it laid the groundwork for Illinois to become the 50th and final state to adopt a concealed carry permitting system. Illinois's "Firearm Concealed Carry Act" was passed in July 2013 and permit applications became available to the public the following January. Nearly 92,000 residents received Illinois Concealed Carry Licenses (ICCLs) in the first year they were available.[40] But these licenses came with as many strings attached as any shall issue system in the country.

Not all Illinois residents are eligible to receive ICCLs.[41] To qualify, an applicant must be 21 years of age and have a valid Firearm Owner's Identification (FOID) card issued by the State of Illinois. Individuals prohibited from receiving a FOID card – and hence an ICCL – include: illegal aliens, those institutionalized for mental health issues in the past five years and the mentally/developmentally disabled, convicted felons, those convicted of domestic battery/violence, and those subject to an active Order of Protection. Other disqualifying conditions for an ICCL are: being convicted of more than one DWI violation or any misdemeanor involving use or threat of physical force/ violence, or being in treatment for alcohol or drug addiction within the last 5 years. Any law enforcement agency also has the opportunity to object to the issuance of an ICCL, which sends the application to the state's Concealed Carry Licensing Board for a decision. The law also provides that the Illinois State Police (ISP) shall object to any application from a person who has five or more arrests for any reasons or three or more arrests for gang-related offenses in the previous seven years.

Applicants who are not disqualified must be fingerprinted and undergo a minimum of 16 hours of training in courses taught by instructors certified by the ISP. At least 12 hours of training takes place in the classroom and covers firearms safety, care and cleaning, marksmanship, and legal aspects of owning, storing, carrying, and transporting firearms. A minimum of 4 hours of instruction in gunhandling must take place on the range, culminating in a 30 round shooting test. Applicants must use a concealable firearm and shoot 10 rounds each from a distance of 5 yards, 7 yards, and 10 yards at a B-27 silhouette target. Of the 30 rounds fired, at least

70 percent must hit anywhere on the body of the target, which measures roughly one foot wide by two feet tall.

Dwayne Beccue of Vanguard Personal Defense in Effingham County teaching an Illinois concealed carry permit class.

Credit: Photo courtesy of Dwayne Beccue

Alex Kogan, a Chicago-based gun trainer who runs Misha Tactical Arms, has taught the Illinois concealed carry class to over 1,000 students since 2013. In that time, he has had only one student that he could not train to a passing level in the course, which he describes as "devastating" to him as an instructor. In fact, most of his students score 100% on the shooting test, both because of the relative ease of the course of fire and the time he spends on the range teaching them to shoot.

Upon receiving an application (including certification of training and a $150 fee for five years), the ISP conducts a background check of the applicant, including using the FBI's National Instant Criminal Background Check System (NICS) and the files of the Department of Human Services relating to mental health and developmental disabilities. If the ISP determines the applicant qualifies, the Illinois Concealed Carry License is issued. To echo Supreme Court Justice Antonin Scalia's 2008 decision in *District of Columbia v. Heller*, however, this does not allow the licensee to "carry any weapon whatsoever in any manner whatsoever and for whatever purpose."

What permits are called sometimes reflect substantive differences. For example, Florida issues a Concealed *Weapon or Firearm* License while North Carolina issues a Concealed *Handgun* License. Florida's permit covers carrying of "a handgun, electronic weapon or device, tear gas gun, knife, or billie."[42] North Carolina's, like most permits nationally, covers only handguns. This is the case in Illinois where the statute defines a handgun as "any device which is designed to expel a projectile or projectiles by the action of an explosion, expansion of gas, or escape of gas that is designed to be held and fired by the use of a single hand." By this definition, an ICCL does not permit concealed carry of long guns or any air, spring, paintball, BB, or similar guns.

All states – whether they are may issue, shall issue, or permitless – limit where private citizens can carry concealed weapons. Illinois's law includes a long list of prohibited places, including (but not limited to): colleges and universities, elementary and secondary schools, pre-school or child care facilities, government buildings and courthouses, jails, hospitals or mental health facilities or nursing homes, public transportation and related facilities, bars and restaurants deriving more than half of profits from alcohol, public gatherings or special events, public playgrounds and parks, casinos and racetracks, stadiums and arenas, public libraries, airports, amusement parks, zoos, museums, nuclear sites, and anywhere firearms are prohibited by federal law. In addition, any "owner of private real property of any type may prohibit the carrying of concealed firearms on the property under his or her control" by "clearly and conspicuously" posting a uniform sign adopted by the ISP.

According to one exasperated recent recipient of an ICCL with whom I spoke, "It seems like there are more places I *can't* carry than places I *can*." She has a point. Even with her license, this Chicago resident cannot legally carry her Smith & Wesson revolver when entering her downtown office building, eating at her favorite restaurants, visiting the Art Institute, walking through Grant Park, or riding the "L." Effectively, she has to leave her gun at home when she leaves for work Monday through Friday, and many times on weekends as well, depending on where she is going.

Another major restriction affecting concealed carry licensees is the use of alcohol or other drugs. According to the Illinois law, "A licensee shall not carry a concealed firearm while under the influence of alcohol, other drug or drugs, intoxicating compound or combination of compounds, or any combination thereof," under standards found in the Illinois Vehicle Code. This means 0.08 blood alcohol content, any amount of evidence of use of marijuana or other controlled substances listed in Illinois law (such as cocaine or methamphetamine), or any substance "that renders the person incapable of driving safely."[43] This actually makes Illinois's permit more liberal than some. In Arizona, North Carolina, and Tennessee, for example, you cannot consume *any* alcohol while carrying a concealed handgun.

As the case of Illinois's concealed carry law suggests, not all concealed carry laws are created equal. Beyond the broad distinction between "shall issue" and "may issue," there is considerable variation from state to state in every aspect of concealed carry: who can carry, and what, where, and when they can carry. Shall issue concealed carry represents a liberalization of American gun laws, but within that broad movement, some states are more liberal than others. Illinois is on the high end of the regulation spectrum.

North Carolina is somewhat more moderate. It requires applicants for concealed carry permits to complete an application, be fingerprinted, pay a fee, and successfully complete 8 hours of "an approved firearms safety and training course which involves the actual firing of handguns and instruction in the laws of this

State governing the carrying of a concealed handgun and the use of deadly force."[44] North Carolina's original 1995 shall issue law was amended in 2013 to allow concealed carry in bars and restaurants where alcohol is sold and consumed, parades and funerals, state and municipal parks, and some educational properties.

On the low end of the regulatory spectrum for shall issue states is Pennsylvania, which does not require applicants to complete any training course. Pennsylvania charges $19 for a permit, valid for five years and requires only that the applicant meet certain qualifying conditions, most of which are required for legally owning a gun in the first place. The earliest state to go shall issue, Washington is also one of the most liberal. This was discovered by msnbc.com reporter Mike Stuckey when he was able to apply for a concealed pistol license from the King County Sheriff's Office in downtown Seattle in just 22 minutes. Like Pennsylvania and many other states, no training course is required to receive a Washington State concealed carry permit.[45]

Whether those who apply for concealed carry permits should have to take a class, what that class should cover, and whether hands-on firearms training should be part of the required curriculum are among the most controversial issues surrounding the liberalization of concealed weapon laws.

Five

STATE VARIATION IN TRAINING REQUIREMENTS

⟡━━━━⟡

Those who oppose liberalized shall issue permitting systems often raise the objection that people should not be able to carry guns in public without "proper training." Jennifer Mascia, a reporter for the Michael Bloomberg backed gun violence reporting initiative, *The Trace*, reviewed the training requirements of the 50 states in February 2016 and found them about evenly divided in terms of a "live-fire" requirement. 24 states and the District of Columbia have a "live-fire" requirement like the ones in Illinois and North Carolina. 25 states are like Pennsylvania and Washington State in not requiring any range time to receive a permit. (Recall that Vermont does not issue permits to carry.) As the headline for Mascia's story in *The Trace* story declares, "25 States Will Let You Carry a Concealed Gun Without Making Sure You Know How to Shoot One." Moreover, existing recognition and reciprocity agreements between states create a situation in which it is possible for people "to criss-cross the country toting concealed guns, without anyone having verified that their aim is true."[46]

This matter is made even worse for proponents of live-fire requirements by the most recent broad movement in the liberalization of concealed carry: permitless carry. A growing number of states – 15 total, including 3 since 2019 – are adopting what might be called "Alaska Carry" (see Table 2).[47] The term refers to the fact that Alaska was the first state, in 2003, to adopt a system in which the government *issues but does not require* concealed carry permits. This means that anyone who can legally possess a gun can carry it concealed in public without a license (although various other restrictions on who, what, where, and when still apply).[48]

Table 2. State Adoption of Permitless Concealed Carry Laws

Year	States
Always	Vermont
2003	Alaska
2010	Arizona, Wyoming
2015	Kansas, Maine, Mississippi
2016	Idaho,[49] Missouri, West Virginia
2017	New Hampshire, North Dakota (residents only)
2018	Arkansas[50]
2019	Kentucky, Oklahoma, South Dakota

Note: Dates in this table are from my own research and Trent Steidley, "Sharing the Monopoly on Violence? Shall-Issue Concealed Handgun License Laws and Responsibilization," *Sociological Perspectives* (2019), Table 1.

Of states that require some course or training, Illinois is among the most stringent. Virginia, by contrast, has a competency requirement, but is among the most liberal in terms of what can satisfy the requirement. Virginia's statute specifies that the circuit court "shall require proof that the applicant has demonstrated competence with a handgun." But the manner in which applicants can demonstrate such competence is extremely broad. Any of the following satisfy the requirement:

1. Completing any hunter education or hunter safety course approved by the Department of

Game and Inland Fisheries or a similar agency of another state;

2. Completing any National Rifle Association firearms safety or training course;

3. Completing any firearms safety or training course or class available to the general public offered by a law-enforcement agency, junior college, college, or private or public institution or organization or firearms training school utilizing instructors certified by the National Rifle Association or the Department of Criminal Justice Services;

4. Completing any law-enforcement firearms safety or training course or class offered for security guards, investigators, special deputies, or any division or subdivision of law enforcement or security enforcement;

5. Presenting evidence of equivalent experience with a firearm through participation in organized shooting competition or current military service or proof of an honorable discharge from any branch of the armed services;

6. Obtaining or previously having held a license to carry a firearm in the Commonwealth or a locality thereof, unless such license has been revoked for cause;

7. Completing any firearms training or safety course or class, including an electronic, video, or online course, conducted by a state-certified or National Rifle Association-certified firearms instructor;

8. Completing any governmental police agency firearms training course and qualifying to carry a firearm in the course of normal police duties; or

9. Completing any other firearms training which the court deems adequate.[51]

In contrast to states like Alaska, Illinois, and North Carolina, whose required courses must have a hands-on weapon handling component and specifically address when a firearm can be used in self-defense, Virginia allows applicants to demonstrate competence and receive a concealed carry permit without either.

To be sure, some of the demonstration methods included in the statute set a fairly high standard for competence in the safe handling of firearms. Of note is #5, which allows the applicant to submit evidence of "experience with a firearm through participation in organized shooting competition" or military service.[52] Under #2, those who attend a National Rifle Association (NRA) "First Shots" course will certainly get some hands-on education in the safe use of a firearm. Even more so, an applicant who takes an NRA Basics of Personal Protection Outside the Home (PPOTH) course will learn "safe, effective and responsible use of a concealed pistol for self-defense outside the home," including live-fire on the range and coverage of laws governing the use of firearms for self-defense. The NRA PPOTH course is costly, however, typically involving a 16-hour time commitment over two days and a cost of $100 to $350 (depending on the instructor), not including ammunition costs or range fees.

This made option #7 attractive to some looking for a low bar, at least through the end of 2020. Applicants could fulfill Virginia's competence requirement through an on-line course. One such course was offered by The Carry Academy (carryacademy.com).[53] A $49.99 fee gave you access to a 30 minute handgun safety video followed by "a quick and easy 20 question test." Upon passing the test with a score of 75 percent or better, you could print out a certificate that satisfies the competence requirement for a Virginia concealed carry permit. If you were among the 1 percent of test-takers who did not pass on your first attempt, you could repeat the test. Another on-line option was Virginia Concealed (virginiaconcealed.com). Unlike the Carry Academy, Virginia Concealed allowed individuals to watch their 40-minute safety course and take their 11 question test free. Once the test was passed (with 8 correct answers, or 73%), the customer had the opportunity to pay $65 to order the certificate necessary to apply for the Virginia concealed carry permit. Among on-line options, the

Concealed Carry Institute (concealed-carry.net) offered the least expensive course that satisfied Virginia's requirement. $29.99 gave you access to a 65 minute video, a 20 question test, and a certificate of completion necessary to apply for the Virginia permit. Apparently this bar was seen as too low for the Virginia legislature, which revised #7 to remove the online option. Effective on 1 January 2021, the code reads: "Completing any in-person firearms training or safety course or class conducted by a state-certified or National Rifle Association-certified firearms instructor."

Of course, as Alex Kogan's extremely low failure rate in Illinois suggests, even those states that have specific live-fire tests do not screen out many applicants. Texas has one of the country's most challenging shooting test for its license to carry. It uses the same B-27 target as Illinois, but adds difficulty by requiring 20 more rounds to be fired (50 total), adding a time limit (e.g., 5 shots in 10 seconds), requiring applicants to shoot 10 of the 50 rounds from 15 yards distance, and awarding more points to more accurate shots. Students get three attempts to earn 175 out of 250 possible points (70%) to pass, something over one million Texans have done since 1995. Karl Rehn of KR Training tells me that in twenty-plus years of teaching over 1,500 of those license-to-carry students, has had just a handful of students not successfully complete the course. In a video for the online "lounge" of Lucky Gunner ammo, gun trainer John Johnston and lounge host Chris Baker demonstrate the low bar represented by mandatory live-fire requirements by shooting and passing the Texas course of fire *while blindfolded.*[54]

John Johnston of Citizens Defense Research shooting the Texas concealed carry permit qualification test blindfolded, with Chris Baker observing.

Credit: Photo Courtesy of Lucky Gunner

For some, the low bar for passing concealed carry courses of fire is itself a compromise, as they believe there should be no course or training requirement imposed for citizens to exercise their Constitutional rights. Groups like the National Association for Guns Rights (NAGR) support permitless carry because they believe "the Constitution is my carry permit." As the NAGR put it in a fundraising letter sent to its millions of Facebook followers in 2016, "No citizen should have to beg the government for a permit before he or she can exercise their Constitutional right to bear arms." Furthermore, the NAGR maintains that "firearms training should be affordable, high-quality, and legally optional."[55] From this perspective, the very idea of a mandatory concealed carry class is offensive. That any training or testing should be *required* is anathema to the exercise of the *right* to keep and bear arms — just as there is no training or tests required to exercise free speech or the right to vote or practice one's religion.

As the NAGR suggests, this is not opposition to training, per se. Voluntary training in the use of firearms and self-defense law is widely embraced and promoted within Gun Culture 2.0.[56] "But concealed carry is a licensing class, not a training class," according to Arkansas gun trainer Rob Jennings. "If gun training is a ladder, a concealed carry course is just walking up to the ladder." Karl Rehn offers a similar perspective in his book with John Daub, *Strategies and Standards for Defensive Handgun Training*. They argue that "state standards aren't realistic minimum performance standards" because they "don't include all the skills the average gun owner should be trained in" if they carry a handgun for self-defense.[57] Perhaps most notably, no state-mandated concealed carry course requires students to draw from concealment, a necessary precondition of using a concealed handgun in self-defense. According to Rehn and Daub, those who teach the NRA Basic Pistol course, which satisfies the concealed carry training requirement in many states, are not even certified by the NRA to teach drawing from a holster if they wanted to go beyond the state minimum, as some trainers do in their concealed carry courses.[58]

The alternative to the present system, from the perspective of some gun trainers, is not to add state mandated requirements where they don't exist or to increase them where they do. "The live-fire training requirement is a red herring," observes the aforementioned blindfolded shooter John Johnston, co-owner of the gun training company Citizens Defense Research and a leading voice in the industry through his syndicated talk-show, "Ballistic Radio." "It's unrealistic to think that I can give you an 8 hour class on a life-saving practice and think that class is going to be meaningful," Johnston continues. "Nothing about those classes teaches you how to carry a gun on a daily basis and defend your life with a gun if the need arises. I would be fine if the state advocated meaningful training, but the amount of time and money that would cost is prohibitive."

Requiring a meaningful training course as a prerequisite for receiving a concealed carry permit would have the unintended − or, perhaps for some, intended − consequence of creating a substantial barrier to the exercise of the right to bear arms, and one that discriminates especially against those who are more socially and economically disadvantaged. Johnston, therefore, like many of his peers in the gun training industry, embraces and promotes voluntary defensive firearms training. Tom Gresham, host of the nationally-syndicated radio program "Gun Talk" repeats almost as a mantra that "your concealed carry class is *not* training." Gresham insists that any responsible gun owner should take *real* training courses, but the government should not require or regulate that training.

Gun Culture 2.0 is not monolithic on this issue, of course. Some believe not only that training should be required to receive a concealed carry permit, but that the training should meet a uniformly high standard. A case is point is a group of concealed carry instructors in California's central valley who were concerned about variation in the quality of instruction permit applicants were receiving under California's decentralized system. As we have already seen, California's implementation of its may issue concealed carry system varies considerably from county to county, from *de facto* "shall issue" to *de facto* "no issue." California's statutory language for the required training course in the early 2010s was also very general in terms of course requirements and gave responsibility to the local licensing authority to approve courses:

> For new license applicants, the course of training for issuance of a license under Section 26150

or 26155 may be any course acceptable to the licensing authority, shall not exceed 16 hours, and shall include instruction on at least firearm safety and the law regarding the permissible use of a firearm.[59]

As a consequence, a concealed carry permit applicant in one county could satisfy the requirement by taking a four-hour course with no range time, and in another county be required to take a 16-hour course with a significant live-fire requirement.

Ken Zachary was among those firearms trainers in California concerned about the lack of clear and consistent standards for concealed carry courses. Zachary's concealed carry courses are approved by the Sheriffs of San Luis Obispo, Fresno, Madera, Tulare, and Kings Counties, and he is also certified to teach the standardized concealed carry curriculum for the State of Utah. His experience teaching the Utah program helped him see the benefit of having a single lesson plan that everyone in the state follows. For a couple of years, he shared his thoughts on the value of standardization with fellow instructors. These peers became the core of the California Concealed Carry Instructor's Group (CCIG), whose chief goal was "to organize CCW [concealed carry weapons] instructors toward common requirements in all California Counties regarding CCW issuance. The idea is to propose uniform lesson plans and training for statewide uniformity and consistency."

This effort gained momentum when Zachary was appointed in 2013 to chair the California Rifle and Pistol Association's (CRPA) Carry Handgun License Committee. Founded in 1875, the CRPA is the state-level analogue of the National Rifle Association. As chair of the Carry Handgun License Committee, Zachary was in a position to advance the goals of the CCIG by having the CRPA sanction the standards it was developing. This would make their adoption by individual county sheriffs or even the California State Sheriffs' Association more likely. In September 2013, a planning meeting drew 50 trainers. As Nick Prizant, a core member of the peer group and the host of the planning session, wrote in his meeting summary,

> Our goal is to set in place a permanent organization responsible for helping to train civilians to responsibly and effectively carry concealed weapons in public. In this day and age of increased violence and danger in the world, we believe in the need for armed citizens. But above all else, these armed citizens need to be well educated, trained, prepared, and SAFE.

Two specific actions to that end would be to establish a teaching standard for concealed carry training courses and to develop an instructor certification process for those who would teach the standardized courses. The end goal was for CRPA Certified Instructors to be teaching CRPA Certified Courses statewide. "What we intend to accomplish," Prizant continued, "has never been done before in the State of California, or anywhere else that we have heard of. We, essentially, are going to make history."

The CCIG decided to charge David Matthews and Ernie Hernandez with developing a concealed handgun license curriculum to present to the CRPA at their board of directors meeting in February 2014. Matthews and Hernandez saw their charge similarly. They did not want to teach courses that just met a minimum standard. "We wanted to raise the bar," Hernandez recalled, sitting in his office at Master at Arms Security Solutions, a private security and training firm he owns and operates. "We wanted people to be *trained*." In early February 2014, just prior to the CRPA board meeting, Matthews circulated to the CCIG the final 18-page draft of the Concealed Handgun License Curriculum. The proposed curriculum observed that being permitted to carry a firearm "entails *grave social responsibility*" and "*makes us duty-bound* to give the matter our deepest thought." Among those responsibilities is to know how to store and use a gun safely, to learn and follow applicable laws, and to have given some thought to the possibility of having to shoot another person.

The curriculum suggested instructors address issues of emotional maturity, such as "being able to differentiate between fear and danger" and "understanding that lethal force is not the solution to every conflict." It also highlighted ways of avoiding life-threatening confrontations. This was anything but a "shoot first and ask questions later" training course.

As robust as the legal, ethical, psychological, and practical aspects of the proposed curriculum were, perhaps its most radical aspect was the live-fire portion – the missing part of concealed carry training that Mascia's story in *The Trace* highlighted. The proposed range element of the curriculum included a prequalification course of fire allowing the instructor to teach and assess the permit applicant's ability to draw a gun from a holster, handle various gun malfunctions, move and shoot, reload, and shoot one handed, seated, and from the hip. Upon successful completion of this prequalification, the applicant would then shoot the 7 stage qualification course of live-fire. This would require a minimum of 60 rounds fired in various manners from various distances and according to different time standards. The proposed course included, at different points in the test, drawing the gun from concealment, shooting one-handed from the hip position, movement to and shooting from behind a barricade, reloading, and shooting while kneeling. To qualify, the applicant would be required get a minimum of 70 percent hits inside the "7 ring" of a B-27 humanoid target. (The 7 ring measures about 16 inches wide and 2 feet tall.)

When Ken Zachary and Nick Prizant presented the CCIG's Concealed Handgun License Curriculum to the CRPA board in February 2014, it was not well-received. According to Prizant, some board members continued to think of the organization as being fundamentally about hunting and target shooting, not self-defense – Gun Culture 1.0 not Gun Culture 2.0. As Ernie Hernandez described them, "They are older than dirt. Oxygen tanks. Walkers." But opposition to the curriculum standardization also came from board members who fully supported the right to bear arms in public. Like the NRA, the CRPA's official position on concealed carry supports permitless carry. These opponents feared that standardizing training across counties under the auspices of the CRPA would not only represent the organization's acceptance of gun regulations, but would also be an invitation to vehemently anti-gun (then) California Attorney General (now Vice President) Kamala Harris to coopt concealed carry training and administer it from the top-down. The proposal went down hard. As Zachary colorfully described it after the fact, "I got my ass handed to me." Zachary, Ernie Hernandez, Nick Prizant, and David Matthews continue to teach concealed carry courses, but the CCIG is dormant, as is the idea of raising the bar for the mandatory concealed carry training course in California.

Concerns about individuals receiving inadequate training notwithstanding, I know of no evidence that states with higher levels of training required to receive concealed carry permits have fewer problems with gun carriers than states with lower training requirements. This may be one reason that some states have recently reduced the length of their mandatory concealed carry classes. In 2013, Texas shortened its class requirement from 10-15 hours to 4-6 hours; in 2014, South Carolina eliminated its eight-hour class requirement (though still requires proof of training); and in 2015, Ohio shortened its required class from 12 to 8 hours. Along with the growing number of states that are allowing or considering permitless carry, these developments are indicative of the continuing liberalization of carry laws and the expanding right to bear arms in late 20th and early 21st century America.[60]

CONCLUSION

⌐━━━━━⌐

A convenient framework for summarizing the broad historical development of concealed weapons laws in the United States just described is this: The 19th century was the century of concealed weapons *prohibitions*. The 20th century was the century of concealed weapons *permits*, with *may issue* permitting systems dominating early in the 20th century, giving way to *shall issue* permitting by the turn of the 21st. Today, concealed carry of handguns in public by ordinary citizens is permissible, although not equally possible, under the law in all 50 states and the District of Columbia (see Table 3).

It is impossible to say whether the trend of gun law liberalization with respect to concealed carry will continue indefinitely into the future. Efforts to pass a national concealed carry reciprocity bill in Congress were emboldened by the election of Donald Trump to the presidency in 2016, with strong backing from the National Rifle Association. Such a law would require that every state in the U.S. recognize the validity of a concealed carry permit from another state. This would put concealed carry licenses on a par with driver's licenses and wedding licenses. Though Rep. Richard Hudson (R-NC) introduced a Concealed Carry Reciprocity Act in both the 115th (2017-2018) and 116th (2019-2020) Congresses, neither bill made much legislative progress. As the Trump administration gives way to the administration of President Joe Biden, national concealed carry reciprocity is unlikely in the near future.

Table 3. State Distribution of Permitting Systems

Permitting System	# of States	States
Permitless carry with no permits available	1	Vermont
Permitless carry with de jure or de facto shall issue	15	Alaska, Arizona, Arkansas, Idaho, Kansas, Kentucky, Maine, Mississippi, Missouri, New Hampshire, North Dakota, Oklahoma, South Dakota, West Virginia, Wyoming

| Shall issue | 25 | Alabama, Colorado, Florida, Georgia, Illinois, Indiana, Iowa, Louisiana, Michigan, Minnesota, Montana, Nebraska, Nevada, New Mexico, North Carolina, Ohio, Oregon, Pennsylvania, South Carolina, Tennessee, Texas, Utah, Virginia, Washington State, Wisconsin |
| May issue | 9 | California, Connecticut, Delaware, Hawaii, Maryland, Massachusetts, New Jersey, New York, Rhode Island |

Note: Following a 2017 D.C. Circuit Court of Appeals decision in *Wrenn v. District of Columbia* and *Grace v. District of Columbia*, the D.C. Metropolitan Police Department no longer requires applicants for concealed carry permits to provide a "good reason." It is, therefore, a shall issue jurisdiction.[61]

At the same time, the invigoration of the gun control movement in the wake of the December 2012 massacre at Sandy Hook Elementary School in Newtown, Connecticut has led to passage of a number of restrictive gun laws by various state and local governments. To date, the Supreme Court of the United States has refused to hear challenges to the constitutionality of these restrictions, like New York State's SAFE Act or the ban on higher capacity magazines in Sunnyvale, California. Although the Supreme Court of the United States has held, in the *Heller* and *McDonald* decisions, that individuals have the right to own handguns, it has not definitively supported the right to carry those in public. Donald Trump's appointment of three justices has certainly given gun rights supporters hope that a more conservative Supreme Court may soon do so.

What cannot be questioned is that Gun Culture 2.0 fosters and is fostered by shall issue permitting and permitless carry. Both of these legal developments make concealed carry in public by ordinary citizens much easier today than any time in the past 150 years.

Finding Up-to-Date Information on Concealed Carry Laws

As concealed carry laws change regularly, the best way to stay current is to consult reliable web sources, which can be updated much more frequently than printed publications. Three sources I rely upon are:

- *Giffords Law Center to Prevent Gun Violence* provides comprehensive gun law summaries for all 50 states and the Washington, DC, including information on gun transfers, gun dealers, gun owner responsibilities, and firearms in public places (smartgunlaws.org).

- *National Rifle Association Institute for Legislative Action (NRA-ILA)* "State Gun Laws" page includes information the Constitution, concealed carry reciprocity, and laws on purchase, possession and carrying of firearms for all 50 states (nraila.org).

- *USA Carry* provides information on requirements to receive a concealed carry permit for all 50 states and Washington, DC, and is known for its interactive permit reciprocity maps (usacarry.com).

Because each source comes at the issue of concealed carry from a different perspective, your best bet is to cross-check these different sources against each other.

NOTES

[1] 1874 law quote from Robert R. Dykstra, *The Cattle Towns* (New York: Knopf, 1968), p. 119. 1876 law from Joseph Blocher, "Firearm Localism," *Yale Law Journal* 123 (October 2013), p. 84n4. Discussion of Dodge City and photo of sign are in Adam Winkler, *Gunfight: The Battle over the Right to Bear Arms in America* (New York: W.W. Norton & Company, 2011), pp. 165-66.

[2] In addition to the account in Winkler's *Gunfight* (pp. 172-73), see also the alternative perspective less friendly to the Earps in Tom Correa's American Cowboy Chronicles blog, "Tombstone's Ordinance No. 9 was Neither Fair Nor Equally Enforced" (8 August 2014), retrieved on 23 November 2020 from http://

www.americancowboychronicles.com/2014/08/
tombstones-ordinance-no9-was-neither.html.

[3] The Earp Ordinance was renumbered as Ordinance
5-5-1 in 1977. See the 12-part account of the
challenge to the Earp Ordinance written by one of
the three plaintiffs, Terry McGahey, on the American
Cowboy Chronicles blog, "The Last Gun Fight – The
Death of Ordinance Number 9" (1 January 2015),
retrieved on 23 November 2020 from http://www.
americancowboychronicles.com/2015/01/editors-
note-re-last-gun-fight-death-of.html. The Arizona
Department of Public Safety "Concealed Weapons &
Permits" webpage (https://www.azdps.gov/services/
public/cwp) provides comprehensive information about
state laws and keeps an updated total of active permits.

[4] See the "Concealed Carry" page of the Kansas Attorney
General's website (retrieved on 25 November 2020
from http://ag.ks.gov/public-safety/concealedcarry).
Residents of both Arizona and Kansas can still choose
to get concealed carry permits from their respective
states, which allow them reciprocity to carry concealed
in a number of other states. Arizona permit holders
can also use them when buying firearms to forego the
NICS background check and can carry in restaurants
that serve alcohol (if the restaurant does not exercise its
right under the law to ban carry), so long as the person
does not drink.

[5] Winkler, *Gunfight*, p. 173.

[6] I do not mean to downplay the significance for all Americans of federal legislation like the Gun Control Act of 1968 and the Brady Handgun Violence Prevention Act of 1993, or United States Supreme Court decisions like *District of Columbia v. Heller* (54 U.S. 570, 2008) and *McDonald v. City of Chicago* (561 U.S. 742, 2010). I simply wish to highlight how much of the action on gun rights and control takes place at the state and local levels. A recent example is the failure of Congress to pass any new gun control laws after the 2012 massacre at Sandy Hook Elementary School in Newtown, Connecticut, but the successful passage of such laws in Colorado, Connecticut, Maryland, and New York. For example, on New York's 2013 SAFE Act, see James B. Jacobs and Zoe Fuhr, *The Toughest Gun Control Law in the Nation: The Unfulfilled Promise of New York's SAFE Act* (New York: NYU Press, 2019).

Similarly, debates over the meaning of the Second Amendment to the Constitution of the United States often overlook the fact that 44 out of 50 states have constitutional provisions protecting the right to keep and bear arms. The six states with no constitutional provision are: California (1850), Iowa (1846), Maryland (1788), Minnesota (1858), New Jersey (1787), and New York (1788) (year of statehood in parentheses).

Only five of the 44 states with provisions make any reference to "militias," the language that most clouds debates over the meaning of the Second Amendment. Many state constitutions make clear that the right to keep and bear arms goes beyond simple militia service in defense against tyranny. Among the earliest is Pennsylvania, which declared more directly in 1790: "The right of the citizens to bear arms in defence of themselves and the State shall not be questioned" (Art. 1, § 21). Connecticut used similar language in 1818: "Every citizen has a right to bear arms in defense of himself and the state" (Art. I, § 15).

Interestingly, several states have recently amended their constitutions to make clear that the right to keep and bear arms is an individual right and not a collective right tied to militia service (a key finding in the Supreme Court's decision in *Heller*). These developments are part of a broader movement, as political scientist John Dinan has shown recently, to expand rights beyond what is guaranteed in the federal constitution. Alaska, for example, initially enacted the Second Amendment language in its 1959 Constitution, but in 1994 added a second clarifying sentence: "A well-regulated militia being necessary to the security of a free state, the right of the people to keep and bear arms shall not be infringed. The individual right to keep and bear arms shall not be denied or infringed by the State or a political subdivision of the State" (Art. I, § 19). See Dinan's

"State Constitutional Amendments and Individual Rights in the Twenty-First Century," *Albany Law Review* 76.4 (2013):2105-140.

Several states that had no constitutional provisions guaranteeing a right to keep and bear arms added these in the last decades of the 20th century, including: Illinois (1970), Virginia (1971), Nevada (1982), New Hampshire (1982), North Dakota (1984), West Virginia (1987), Delaware (1987), Nebraska (1988), and Wisconsin (1998). The language of these state constitutional provisions are often very similar and all seek to make the point that the right to keep and bear arms is an individual right. See Eugene Volokh, "State Constitutional Rights to Keep and Bear Arms," *Texas Rev. of Law & Politics* 11 (2006):191-217.

[7] In addition to my blog (http://www.gunculture2point0. com), I have also published scholarly articles on Gun Culture 2.0, including "The Sociology of U.S. Gun Culture," *Sociology Compass* 11:7 (2017):e12497, doi: 10.1111/soc4.12497; "'The First Rule of Gunfighting Is Have a Gun': Technologies of Concealed Carry in Gun Culture 2.0," pp. 167–93 in *The Lives of Guns*, edited by J. Obert, A. Poe, and A. Sarat (New York: Oxford University Press, 2019); "The Rise of Self-Defense in Gun Advertising: The American Rifleman, 1918-2017," pp. 9–27 in *Gun Studies: Interdisciplinary Approaches to Politics, Policy, and Practice*, edited by J. Carlson, K.

Goss, and H. Shapira. New York: Routledge, 2019), with Sebastian L. Ivory and Paul C. Yamane; and "Targeted Advertising: Documenting the Emergence of Gun Culture 2.0 in Guns Magazine, 1955–2019," *Palgrave Communications* 6:1 (2020):1–9 (doi: 10.1057/ s41599-020-0437-0).

[8] Craig R. Whitney, *Living with Guns: A Liberal's Case for the Second Amendment* (New York: PublicAffairs, 2012), Chapter 2. See also Joyce Lee Malcolm, *To Keep and Bear Arms: The Origins of an Anglo-American Right* (Cambridge, MA: Harvard University Press, 1994).

[9] Clayton E. Cramer, *Armed America: The Remarkable Story of How and Why Guns Became As American As Apple Pie* (Nashville: Thomas Nelson, 2006), p. 236. De Tocqueville anecdote from Whitney, *Living with Guns*, p. 107.

[10] The Kentucky Supreme Court decision in *Bliss v. Commonwealth, 2 Litt. (Ky.) 90, 13 Am. Dec. 251* is discussed in Clayton Cramer, *Concealed Weapon Laws of the Early Republic: Dueling, Southern Violence, and Moral Reform* (Westport, CT: Praeger, 1999), p. 143.

[11] Cramer, *Concealed Weapon Laws of the Early Republic.* Given the racist origins and consequences of many restrictive laws over the course of American history, a simple explanation for the rise of concealed weapon laws in slave states is that they were meant to control the black population. But prior to the 14th amendment,

Cramer argues, race-specific laws were common, and so the fact that the concealed weapon laws were written in race-neutral language suggests that something else was driving these laws. That something else can be found in the subtitle to the book: *Dueling, Southern Violence, and Moral Reform.*

[12] Robert M. Ireland, "The Problem of Concealed Weapons in Nineteenth-Century Kentucky," *Register of the Kentucky Historical Society* 91 (1993), p. 372, quoted in Cramer, *Concealed Weapon Laws of the Early Republic*, p. 57. Louisiana Supreme Court quoted in Whitney, *Living With Guns*, p. 112.

[13] Lee Kennett and James LaVerne Anderson, *The Gun in America: The Origins of a National Dilemma* (Westport, CT: Praeger, 1975), p. 156.

[14] Kennett and Anderson, *The Gun in America*, pp. 148, 147, 179-80.

[15] Kennett and Anderson, *The Gun in America*, p. 169.

[16] Kennett and Anderson, *The Gun in America*, pp. 170-71. "Promiscuous toting" is from NRA President Karl Frederick, testifying on the 1934 National Firearms Act, quoted in Frank Smyth, *The NRA: The Unauthorized History* (New York: Flatiron Books, 2020), p. 51.

[17] Kennett and Anderson, *The Gun in America*, pp. 172-75.

[18] James Bryce, *The American Commonwealth* (New York: Macmillan, 1889), p. 515.

[19] On Uniform Firearms Act see John Brabner-Smith, "Firearm Regulation," *Law and Contemporary Problems* 1:4 (1934):400-414, and Jeffrey R. Snyder, "Fighting Back: Crime, Self-Defense, and the Right to Carry a Handgun," *Cato Policy Analysis* No. 284 (October 22, 1997), retrieved on 25 November 2020 from https://www.cato.org/publications/policy-analysis/fighting-back-crime-selfdefense-right-carry-handgun.

Brian Anse Patrick, *Rise of the Anti-Media: In-Forming America's Concealed Weapon Carry Movement* (Lanham, MD: Lexington Books, 2010), p 13. Although written in a universalistic language, Patrick argues that these restrictions were powerfully motivated by racism, xenophobia, and class bias. In Patrick's words, "What discretionary systems provided in this low information environment was a system where the masses, the undifferentiated nobodies comprising the working or lower classes, or marginal races, or those beyond the known limits of civilized society were excluded by subjecting them to virtually unattainable levels of proof to establish need. . . . The 'need' in these need-based licensing systems really translates as 'personhood': the respectable, the propertied, the most viable nodes of the social network. The wisdom of the system was that it was exclusionary in the desired direction, while at the same time appearing fair and uniformly objective in its mechanics" (p. 32).

[20] On "may issue" permitting, Clayton E. Cramer and David B. Kopel, "'*Shall* Issue': The New Wave of Concealed Handgun Permit Laws," *Tennessee Law Review* 62 (1994-95), p. 681.

[21] Connecticut is difficult to classify as clearly may issue vs. shall issue. Grossman and Lee, for example, classify Connecticut as shall issue since 1969 ("May Issue versus Shall Issue," Contemporary Economic Policy 26 [April 2008], Table 1, p. 203), while Trent Steidley includes it among his may issue states ("Sharing the Monopoly on Violence? Shall-Issue Concealed Handgun License Laws and Responsibilization," *Sociological Perspectives* [2019], Table 1). Wikipedia classifies Connecticut as shall issue "in practice" and offers this note of clarification: "Connecticut law specifies that CCW licenses be granted on a May issue basis, but the state's courts have established that issuing authorities must grant CCW licenses on a Shall issue basis for applicants who meet all statutory qualifications, as unlike other May issue states Connecticut law does not contain a requirement for the applicant to show 'necessary and proper reason' for obtaining a license" (retrieved on 24 November 2020 from http://en.wikipedia.org/wiki/Concealed_carry_in_the_United_States). According to Cramer and Kopel, "While Connecticut's concealed

weapon permit law does provide an appeal process that appears to be weighted in favor of law-abiding citizens, who wish a permit, there is nothing explicit in the statute that requires a permit to be issued" ("'*Shall* Issue,'" p. 690n.41). The Giffords Law Center to Prevent Gun Violence (retrieved on 24 November 2020 from https:// giffords.org/lawcenter/gun-laws/policy-areas/guns-in-public/concealed-carry/) and the United States Government Accountability Office report, *Gun Control: States' Laws and Requirements for Concealed Carry Permits Vary across the Nation* (GAO-12-717, July 2012) both list Connecticut as may issue.

[22] John R. Lott and Rujun Wang, "Concealed Carry Permit Holders Across the United States: 2020," 2 October 2020. Retrieved on 17 November 2020 from https://papers.ssrn.com/abstract=3703977.

[23] Patrick, *Rise of the Anti-Media*. On New York permit holders, see William Bastone, "Born to Gun; 65 Big Shots with Licenses to Carry," *Village Voice*, September 29, 1987, quoted in Cramer and Kopel, "'*Shall* Issue," p. 684. On Santa Clara County, Robert Salonga, "How a really big check unraveled a well-oiled patronage system with Santa Clara County concealed-gun permits" (20 September 2020), retrieved on 24 November 2020 from https://www.mercurynews.com/2020/09/20/how-a-really-big-check-unraveled-a-well-oiled-patronage-

system-with-santa-clara-county-concealed-gun-permits.

[24] Superior Court of Delaware instructions for an initial permit retrieved on 25 November 2020 from http://courts.delaware.gov/forms/download.aspx?ID=33278. Data on Delaware permits from Lott and Wang, "Concealed Carry Permit Holders across the United States: 2020."

[25] See Steve Garnass, "Cops Get Tougher on Gun Permits," *Denver Post*, April 24, 1988, p. A1, quoted in Snyder, "Fighting Back."

[26] Note: The Calguns Foundation is now the California Gun Rights Foundation. See Calguns Foundation letter to San Francisco Sheriff Michael Hennessey dated 31 May 2011, retrieved on 25 November 2020 from http://www.scribd.com/doc/148649125/CGF-Letter-to-San-Francisco-re-Handgun-Carry-Policy-5-31-11, and Calguns Foundation "Sunshine Initiative Update (Part 2)," retrieved on 25 November 2020 from https://www.cagunrights.org/cgf-and-carry-in-california-sunshine-initiative-update-part-2. The effort to force the San Francisco Sheriff's Department at least to follow the law, even if the result is still no licenses, was part of a broader effort the Calguns Foundation launched called the Carry License Compliance and Sunshine Initiative. See 18 October 2010 press release, retrieved on 25 November 2020 from https://www.cagunrights.

org/calguns-foundation-announces-firearms-carry-licensing-compliance-and-education-program-files-lawsuit-against-ventura-county-sheriff-for-failure-t-o-disclose-public-records-2. According to Calguns, the initiative "is a grassroots education and litigation campaign designed to: Procure and publish objective carry license-related records and other data acquires from licensing authorities and the DOJ (going to actual issuance/denial and the contours of policies, both as-written and as-applied, like local application policies, good cause statements, and reported statistics); Force licensing authorities to comply with state statutes, legal precedent, and the Constitution; Track and monitor local practices; Support applicants and licensees; and, Develop and promulgate materials related to the above."

[27] According to a 2015 story on the Center for Investigative Reporting's *Reveal* website, there are only two active concealed carry permits for the 700,000-plus adult residents of San Francisco, both issued by the City of San Francisco Police Chief. The San Francisco Sheriff's Department serves the geographically coterminous City and County of San Francisco along with the San Francisco Police Department. Matt Drange, "Want to carry a concealed gun? Live in Sacramento, not San Francisco," *Reveal*, (12 June 2015), retrieved on 25 November 2020 from https://www.revealnews. org/article/want-to-carry-a-concealed-gun-live-in-sacramento-not-san-francisco/.

²⁸ Tehama County Sheriff's Office "Concealed Weapons Permits" page, retrieved on 17 November 2020 from https://tehamaso.org/administration/licenses-permits/concealed-weapons. Shasta County data from Drange, "Want to carry a concealed gun?" Highest rate in the state from Hudson Sangree and Phillip Reese, "Concealed gun permits soar in Sacramento County," *The Sacramento Bee* (23 April 2016), retrieved on 17 November 2020 from https://www.sacbee.com/news/local/article73538112.html.

²⁹ See data from California Department of Justice's Bureau of Firearms for 2014 reported by Drange, "Want to carry a concealed gun?"

³⁰ Patrick, *Rise of the Anti-Media*, p. 37. Although Second Amendment advocates highlight the right not just to keep but also to bear arms, the prevailing legal opinion in the United States holds that the government has the authority to regulate the bearing of arms in public. According to U.S. Supreme Court Justice Antonin Scalia's majority decision in the landmark case *District of Columbia v. Heller* (2008), "Like most rights, the Second Amendment right is not unlimited. It is not a right to keep and carry any weapon whatsoever in any manner whatsoever and for whatever purpose: For example, concealed weapons prohibitions have been upheld under the Amendment or state analogues."

³¹ Cramer and Kopel, "'Shall Issue,'" p. 687.

[32] Lawrence Northwood, Richard Westgard, and Charles Barb, Jr., "Law-Abiding One-Man Armies." *Society* 16:1 (1978):69-74.

[33] Cramer and Kopel, "'*Shall* Issue,'" p. 687. See also Grossman and Lee, "May Issue Versus Shall Issue."

[34] Smyth, *The NRA*; Winkler, *Gunfight*, Chapter 3; Yamane, "Sociology of U.S. Gun Culture."

[35] Georgia passed a concealed carry law in 1976 which some (like GeorgiaCarry.org) consider to be a shall issue law (see http://www.georgiacarry.org/cms/georgias-carry-laws-explained/history-of-georgias-carry-laws, accessed 24 November 2020). In 1989, the Georgia Attorney General clarified the ambiguous carry law by maintaining that judges must issue permits to anyone who does not have a disqualifying condition.

[36] Prior to its legalization of permitless carry in 2017, New Hampshire was difficult to classify as either may issue or shall issue. The term "shall issue" appears in its statute, but other language suggests discretion on the part of the issuing authority to determine that "the applicant is a suitable person to be licensed." It may be best classified today as permitless carry allowed with a *de facto* shall issue permitting system in place.

Although Grossman and Lee ("May Issue versus Shall Issue") count New Hampshire as shall issue as of 1959, Cramer and Kopel disagree. Cramer and

Kopel note that they had been "repeatedly told by New Hampshire gun owners that concealed handgun permit issuance is non-discretionary in the Granite State. However, while New Hampshire authorities may issue permits readily, there is nothing in the statutes that requires them to do so" ("'*Shall* Issue,'" p. 690n.41). Indeed, the text of the New Hampshire statute makes this clear. It reads, in part, that the designated authority upon application "shall issue a license to such applicant authorizing the applicant to carry a loaded pistol or revolver in this state for not less than 4 years from the date of issue, if it appears that the applicant has good reason to fear injury to the applicant's person or property or has any proper purpose, and that the applicant is a suitable person to be licensed. Hunting, target shooting, or self-defense shall be considered a proper purpose. The license shall be valid for all allowable purposes regardless of the purpose for which it was originally issued" (Title XII, Chapter 159, Section 159:6; retrieved on 25 November 2020 from http://www.gencourt.state. nh.us/rsa/html/XII/159/159-6.htm). The "proper purpose" language is sufficiently broad as to allow most applicants to qualify, but there remains unqualified language specifying that "the applicant is a suitable person to be licensed."

[37] Cramer and Kopel, "'*Shall* Issue,'" p. 696.

[38] Among social scientists studying the patterns of state passage of liberalized concealed carry laws, Trent Steidley has contributed the most. He finds that states with a *lower* percentage of Black population, *less* economic inequality, and *higher* percentages of college graduates are *less* likely to liberalize their concealed carry laws. States in the South, with male governors, Republican legislatures, a high percentage of NRA members are *more* likely to liberalize their carry laws. The effect of NRA membership is especially pronounced in states with Republican governors and in which the policy "mood" favors gun rights. States with *fewer* police officers and that spend *less* money on law enforcement per capita are *more* likely to pass liberal carry laws. See Trent Steidley, "Big Guns or Big Talk? How the National Rifle Association Matters for Conceal Carry Weapons Laws," *Mobilization: An International Quarterly* 23:1 (2018):101–25; Chad A. Malone and Trent Steidley, "Determinants of Variation in State Concealed Carry Laws, 1970–2016," *Sociological Forum* 34:2 (2019):434–57; and Trent Steidley, "Sharing the Monopoly on Violence? Shall-Issue Concealed Handgun License Laws and Responsibilization," *Sociological Perspectives* (2019).

[39] Lott and Wang estimate 19,482,206 concealed carry permit holders in "Concealed Carry Permit Holders Across the United States: 2020," p. 19.

[40] *Chicago Tribune* story on concealed carry permits in Illinois, 16 January 2015, retrieved on 25 November 2020 from http://www.chicagotribune.com/news/local/breaking/chi-police-2014-concealedcarry-permits-in-illinois-top-91000-20150116-story.html

[41] Information on Illinois law are from the text of Illinois Public Act 098-0063, retrieved on 25 November 2020 from http://www.ilga.gov/legislation/publicacts/98/PDF/098-0063.pdf, and Illinois State Police Firearms Services Bureau Concealed Carry License page, retrieved on 25 November 2020 from https://www.ispfsb.com/Public/CCL.aspx.

[42] Florida Statutes, Title XLVI, Chapter 790, Sec. 790.001, retrieved 25 November 2020 from http://www.leg.state.fl.us/statutes/index.cfm?App_mode=Display_Statute&Search_String=&URL=0700-0799/0790/Sections/0790.001.html.

[43] Illinois Compiled Statutes 625 ILCS 5 Illinois Vehicle Code, Section 11-501, retrieved on 25 November 2020 from http://law.onecle.com/illinois/625ilcs5/11-501.html.

[44] North Carolina General Statute §14-415.12 charged the North Carolina Criminal Justice Education and Training Standards Commission with creating guidelines for courses that would meet the statutory requirement, which were published as Section 09F.0100 of Title 12 of the North Carolina Administrative Code (see

http://reports.oah.state.nc.us/ncac/title%2012%20 -%20justice/chapter%2009%20-%20criminal%20 justice%20education%20and%20training%20 standards/subchapter%20f/subchapter%20f%20rules. html, retrieved on 25 November 2020).

[45] The permit arrived in the mail a month later. Mike Stuckey, "22 Minutes for a Concealed-Weapon Permit," retrieved on 25 November 2020 from https://www. nbcnews.com/id/wbna35839541.

[46] Retrieved on 25 November 2020 from http:// www.thetrace.org/2016/02/live-fire-training-not-mandatory-concealed-carry-permits/.

[47] I owe this term to a gun culture friend, Matthew Carberry.

[48] Although the specifics of the laws vary, in 24 states *openly* carrying a handgun without a permit is legal, and in 39 states there are no restrictions on openly carrying long guns in public without a permit. For example, despite banning concealed carry from 1879 to 1995, North Carolina has never banned open carry nor required a permit to do so. See Wikipedia page on "Open carry in the United States" (retrieved on 25 November 2020 from https://en.wikipedia.org/wiki/ Open_carry_in_the_United_States) and Giffords Law Center to Prevent Gun Violence on "Open Carry" (retrieved on 25 November 2020 from https://giffords.

org/lawcenter/gun-laws/policy-areas/guns-in-public/
open-carry/).

[49] Initial law applied only to Idaho residents was
expanded to include all U.S. citizens in 2020.

[50] Following a 2018 decision by the Arkansas Court
of Appeals in *Taff v. State* (2018 Ark. App. 488)
(https://opinions.arcourts.gov/ark/courtofappeals/
en/346005/1/document.do, retrieved on 25 November
2020), the NRA-ILA and other pro-gun rights
organizations recognized Arkansas as an open carry
state (retrieved on 25 November 2020 from https://
www.nraila.org/gun-laws/state-gun-laws/arkansas/).
As the sections of the Arkansas Code that cover
concealed carry have not yet been amended, however,
gun control organizations like the Giffords Law Center
to Prevent Gun Violence continue to classify Arkansas as
a shall issue permitting state (retrieved on 25 November
2020 from https://giffords.org/lawcenter/state-laws/
concealed-carry-in-arkansas/).

[51] According to §18.2-308.02 of the Code of Virginia,
retrieved on 25 November 2020 from http://law.lis.
virginia.gov/vacode/18.2-308.02/.

[52] The language in this section of Virginia's Code is
taken directly from Florida's statute, and also appears
in Idaho's law.

[53] See one course review by "Jeremy S." on The Truth About Guns, retrieved on 25 November 2020 from http://www.thetruthaboutguns.com/2015/04/jeremy-s/carry-academy-online-ccw-course/.

[54] Johnston scored 78% (195/250) and Baker score 76% (191/250). From "Shooting a Carry Permit Test Blindfolded" (23 April 2019), retrieved on 25 November 2020 from https://www.luckygunner.com/lounge/shooting-a-carry-permit-test-blindfolded/.

[55] Facebook fundraising letter retrieved on 25 November 2020 from http://nagr.org/concarryfb.htm. NAGR on firearms training from "Who's Who in the World of Guns Rights Organizations," retrieved on 25 November 2020 from https://www.outdoornews.com/2016/01/07/whos-who-in-the-world-of-guns-rights-organizations/.

[56] My collected blog posts about the civilian gun training industry/community can be found at: https://gunculture2point0.wordpress.com/2020/04/20/gun-culture-2-0-posts-on-the-private-citizen-or-civilian-gun-training-industry-or-community/.

[57] Karl Rehn and John Daub, *Strategies and Standards for Defensive Handgun Training* (KR Training, LLC, 2019), p. 5.

[58] Although the NRA Basic Pistol Instructor Certification does not certify them to teach holster use, some NRA Basic Pistol instructors are also certified to teach NRA Personal Protection Outside the Home classes, which

do involve drawing from a holster. Rehn also observes that although it is possible to teach beyond what is required in a state-mandated course, competition with other Texas LTC instructors tends to lead to a reduction in what is taught to the minimum required. See Rehn and Daub, *Strategies and Standards for Defensive Handgun Training*, pp. 72-73, 10.

Since its (now defunct) Carry Guard debacle – which included training in addition to "insurance" – the NRA has debuted a new CCW specific course. See "NRA Launches 50-State NRA CCW Course," retrieved on 25 November 2020 from https://www.americanrifleman. org/articles/2019/6/5/nra-launches-50-state-nra-ccw-course/. If successful, this course will reinforce the NRA's status as a quasi-regulatory agency governing concealed carry training in the United States. See my blog post, "The National Rifle Association as Thousands of Spider Monkeys, Not an 800-Pound Gorilla" (https:// gunculture2point0.wordpress.com/2015/10/01/ the-national-rifle-association-as-thousands-of-spider-monkeys-not-an-800-pound-gorilla/), which reflects on lessons learned from Jennifer Carlson's book, *Citizen-Protectors: The Everyday Politics of Guns in an Age of Decline* (New York: Oxford University Press, 2015).

[59] This statutory language was adopted in 2011, and amended slightly more specific language that required the minimum concealed carry course to be 8 hours long

and have a live-fire component (see https://leginfo. legislature.ca.gov/faces/billTextClient.xhtml?bill_ id=201120120SB610, retrieved on 25 November 2020). The more specific language that was removed in 2011 was subsequently reinstated in 2018, so that the California code was the same on 1 January 2019 as it was on 1 January 2011 (see http://192.234.214.85/faces/ billTextClient.xhtml?bill_id=201720180AB2103, retrieved on 25 November 2020).

[60] David Barer, "State law shortens concealed-handgun courses, but will students be prepared?" *Dallas Morning News* (2 September 2013), retrieved on 25 November 2020 from https://www.dallasnews.com/news/ politics/2013/09/02/state-law-shortens-concealed- handgun-courses-but-will-students-be-prepared/; Alan Johnson, "Less-strict gun rules start in Ohio today," *The Columbus Dispatch* (23 March 2015), retrieved on 25 November 2020 from https://www.dispatch.com/ article/20150323/NEWS/303239722; Ben Hallman, "South Carolina Legalizes Concealed Weapons in Bars," *Huffington Post* (11 February 2014), retrieved on 25 November 2020 from https://www.huffpost.com/ entry/guns-in-bars_n_4768884.

[61] DC Metropolitan Police Department, "Applying for a License to Carry a Handgun," retrieved on 25 November 2020 from https://mpdc.dc.gov/page/ applying-license-carry-handgun.